Mystery Monsters

A game for two or more players

David Drew

RIGBY

How to use this book

Some of the monsters in this book are a bit scary. But remember they're much smaller than you and most of them are harmless.

With each picture there are some clues. Use the clues to guess the animal.

When you know the answers, try out this book on a friend.

At the beach

I have no ears and
I cannot hear.
I have ten legs and
I can run sideways.
What am I?

Answer: Crab

Find me on page 14

Under a leaf

I'm as big as your hand and sometimes I bite.
I have eight eyes and eight legs.
What am I?

Answer: spider

Find me on page 14

On a flower

I have no bones and I have no teeth. Once I chewed leaves but now I suck flowers. What am I?

Answer: Butterfly

Find me on page 14

On the grass

I have hooks on
my legs for catching
insects.
I am watching you
with my five eyes.
What am I?

Answer:
Praying mantis

Find me on
page 15

On a tree trunk

I used to live under the ground. Now I am ready to spread my wings.
I have a long beak for sucking juices.
What am I?

Answer: Cicada

Find me on page 15

In the garden

I have sixteen legs and twelve eyes. When I grow up I'll grow some wings. What am I?

Answer: Caterpillar

Find me on page 15

Near a stream

I used to swim
but now I can fly.
I'm one of the fastest
insects alive.
What am I?

Answer: Dragonfly

Find me on page 15

Inside a tree	In the water

I'm knobbly and scaly and I have elbows on my feelers.

What am I?

I'm soft and squashy and I can light up at night.

What am I?

Answer: Weevil

Find us on page 16

Answer: Comb jelly

In the sea

I have ten legs for walking and six legs for swimming.
I can split open my skin and climb out.
What am I?

Answer: shrimp

Find me on page 16

On your window at night

I can taste you
with my feet
and hear you
with my fur.
I fly at night.
What am I?

Answer:

Moth

Find me on
page 16

Here I am

↑ cover: tube worm   ↑ p. 4: crab
↓ p. 5: spider   ↓ p. 6: butterfly

14

Here I am

↑ p. 7: praying mantis   ↑ p. 8: cicada
↓ p. 9: caterpillar   ↓ p. 10: dragonfly

Here I am

↑ p. 11 (L): weevil
↓ p. 12: shrimp

↑ p. 11 (R): comb jelly
↓ p. 13: moth

16